T0166555

CHEER UP, JAY RITCHIE

POEMS BY JAY RITCHIE

Coach House Books | Toronto

first edition

Published with the generous assistance of the Canada Council for the Arts and the Ontario Arts Council. Coach House Books also acknowledges the support of the Government of Canada through the Canada Book Fund and the Government of Ontario through the Ontario Book Publishing Tax Credit.

LIBRARY AND ARCHIVES CANADA CATALOGUING IN PUBLICATION

Ritchie, Jay Winston, 1990-, author
        Cheer up, Jay Ritchie / poems by Jay Ritchie.

Issued in print and electronic formats.
ISBN 978-1-55245-353-7 (softcover).

        I. Title.

PS8635.I777C54 2017   C811'.6   C2017-905078-8

Cheer Up, Jay Ritchie is available in other formats: ISBN 978 1 77056 529 6 (EPUB), ISBN 978 1 77056 530 2 (PDF).

Purchase of the print version of this book entitles you to a free digital copy. To claim your ebook of this title, please email sales@chbooks.com with proof of purchase. (Coach House Books reserves the right to terminate the free digital download offer at any time.)

TABLE OF CONTENTS

WHAT LISPECTOR DID WITH THE ROSE

One day in the middle distant future I will put it down plainly.

Honeysuckle and a guard dog.

Red light from my neighbour's shed.

Already vapour.

I might be mistaken for fireflies.

If so, all the better.

O I eat tangerines.

O I listen to music from the United States.

In the beginning there were two stars.

What Lispector did with the rose.

She can be counted on for that.

In the beginning, two stars.

One for my future.

One for your future.

They got rained on and collapsed.

I love today so much.

Even Hapag-Lloyd shipping containers.

O I make so much sense all the time.

DOG EAT DOG

The mall has secret tunnels
that lead to other parts of the mall. Meet me
by the solar-powered trash compactor.

I get off on being young. I am older
than myself.
Am I 'Goin' to Acapulco'?

White guilt is unhelpful.
I traded *In Utero*
for 26 oz. of Bombay Sapphire.

I was young, I lived in a Doggy Dog world.
Post-postmodern subjects
are renovating the imitation.

Inside of me there is another me
asking for more money. A band called Suuns
and a band called Sunn O))).

There's a bottle of vodka
in the basement. The optometrist asked Monica
some very personal questions.

I would love some
Percocet. Nothing. Nothing. A pigeon.
Its foot. Nothing.

This is really intelligent,
like 'slutting it up' in my twenties. I watch
shafts of light slant through the trees.

I watch a fly struggle to escape from a web
and come up with a good analogy
for getting into an argument on Facebook.

How much money
do I need?
That fruit plate is stunning.

WATER TOWER

I held my hands in the shape of a book
and wrote a novel in blackberries.
They were the colour of night
in an advertisement.
I carried evening the way
a deaf composer carries thunder
from piano to pit.
My opera announced a vacancy
after it bulled through plywood,
which was the room divider.
Corrupt, I love watching trains
divide the neighbourhood.
When I listened to my voicemail,
I conceived of my body
and moved to St. Henri
as a tower of water.
The fruit stand owner
thought the weather was appropriate
for sleeping, I took his advice.

IN WATERMELON SUGAR

At the top of the hill is the Canadian
Centre for Architecture.

Dental school was just around the corner.

The sheer possibility. I had a good time
hunting salamanders. When Allen Ginsberg

went to Prague the kids were excited!
The detective in cop clothes wants to know
if every tree is lifted

by the nuclear power plant in the sky.
I drank red wine and coped like an adult.

I cried in my dad's suv.

My mom was impressed that I walked?
Home is a fishing rod

that catches the remaining trout in me. I am afraid
to know the bottom of a body
of water. Anybody. Ali took me

to a park that was a square.
I guess she wanted to ruin Montreal.

One thing death and winning
the lottery have in common
is suddenness.

THE WAITING ROOM

requires a series
of short commitments,
the way Highway
1 needs to
be reimagined after
each pirouetting pine
tree, the way
an extension cord
needs to be
wound eight times
before it is
a noose. I
made a promise
in the driveway
not to go
inside until I
had sunk twenty-three
baskets consecutively. Light
has a special
way of falling
into polygons in
the waiting room.
The sewage truck
is idling outside
the walk-in clinic
beside the public
library. People fall
out of my
life like oranges
off the back
of a truck.
Residents of Heatherglen
Housing Co-operative Ltd.
were not informed.

A paint stain
on the window
starts to look
modern. The rehabbed
juvenile delinquent said,
Building a house
is just a
series of small
tasks that amount
to something big.
I was out
there in the
driveway until dark.
Here, the Venn
diagram made by
the water's surface
and lip of
the glass. It
was a promise
I made to
luck so that
luck would be
promised to me.

STAY IN TOUCH, DON'T FORGET TO WRITE, YOUR
FRIENDS ARE HERE FOR YOU AND ALWAYS WILL BE

The stores had changed
and so had I.
We were different together.

I walked from east to west inside,
which afforded a more accurate
view of the city.

Flights to Jamaica were on sale
and so were flights to Edmonton,
but the ads were different:

one used pictures,
the other used numbers.
A T-shirt convinced me

of Los Angeles.
A mother pushing her stroller
is a right triangle.

Every art history book
had the same narrative:
start with purity,

then end with laziness
and good timing.
Sears, I keep getting lost in Sears.

AS IF WE AREN'T MASSIVE

Midas running a golden stick
along the fence and beyond
into the day all May,
participating in money
the way children do.
Enjoy Breaking Through
with the sun making
a sun sound
and water becoming
aware of samsara
120 miles above
Europa, Jupiter's
special moon.
My affection bought
a ladder, it showed me things
I had never seen! Before!,
some landman from green Alberta
screamed on the logging road.

WITH WILD ABANDON AND UNCOMMON HOPE WE SET OUT ON OUR JOURNEY

I don't know why I write
about my past.
I would rather write
about my pasta,
here, in front of me,
covered in red
sauce made from
pomodoro and *sale*.

Fact: Frank O'Hara took
a psychology class taught
by Professor Boring in 1946.

The clocks go ahead
one hour today.
Packets of information
called bytes
ripped through wires and air
to make an adjustment
on my smartphone.
I woke up in a bedroom
more orange than grey.
Life is a game show, I thought,
opening Bedroom Door No. 1.

I anticipated a gold wrapper
on my way to Caffè Italia,
but found only melting snow
coughing up wet trash
into our beatific faces.

Can I trust my love
instinct anymore?

Did I do it justice buying
cat food on speed?

I contemplated this
while my paycheque cooed,
If you continue to leave
before things get better
you will exist in a constant
state of departure.

Fact: The pasta is in a bowl
of unknown material.

I made pasta because
I wanted to avoid the actual
conditions of my life:
the commercial break,
the promised prize money,
my private unfair judgements
about his suit or her choice
of earrings, the wheel of fortune.

Today my surroundings are
an endless stream of winnings.

For example, this morning
I was a beautiful girl
named Carissa.
All the sunshine had me
in the mood for budgeting.
The wind was blowing my hair around.

I DON'T WANT TODAY

I don't want today:
white brick, nests, or clarity.
You're a respected poet,
I respect you,
but
I miss the rain. And
I miss
falling asleep watching *Sailor Moon*.
All the words are there,
some of them say
'Computer Sciences' –
this grass is not a meadow
either.

MULTI-LEVEL MARKETING

What it meant to be skateboarding
in the partying shadow of a tree,
I don't know.

I don't

take advice from the Lululemon bag,
Do One Thing a Day
That Scares You,

even though I feel poptimistic.

I don't

want yoga pants, and besides,
There Is No Such Thing
As Ethical Consumption
Under Capitalism.

I read that on Tumblr
while working at the self-storage,
dizzy with love and disappointment
like my past self in Paris,

charging my phone
at the Mac Store across from the Louvre,
searching for x on the internet.
(Later x appeared
at a flea market in Berlin.
It was so thrilling to manifest x!
I bought x.)

But it's always like that –

truth's long striped tail

moving just out of sight,

dropping braids of synthetic purple hair
for me to collect in July.

I'm not trying

for synchronicity
or surprise pagodas,
though I feel numinous
at the SAAQ,

exceeding everyone's expectations,
like water in a Coca-Cola bottle.

In a Society That Profits from Your Self-Doubt,
Liking Yourself Is a
Rebellious Act.

I read that on Tumblr
under the obelisk at the Saddledome,
where I learned contradictory symbolism
can express germane banking info.

I committed to an act of self-love.
I bought tear-resistant pants
just in case

I'm not

a good guy underneath it all,
being honest in discreet doses
to underpaid retail employees.

I'm not

one of them
and I never have been,
masculinity wouldn't let me

say, *I need help*,
so I built a rampart of philosophy,
In solitude one finds oneself –

even if what I found
was minimum wage
at Subway restaurants
in jonquil Cardiff

and that my work ethic
is a poor excuse for personality,
though I feel high
at a third wave
one hour in.

I can imagine a better world.
I'm a good fit for this position.
I have promoter experience.

Here come the horticulturalists,

ending another kalpa
while I sit at the computer
taking every Vegas ad for granted.

A Truly Rich Man Is One Whose Children
Run into His Arms Even When His
Hands Are Empty,

Mark Bradford titled a mixed-media
work I saw hungover
in Chicago in 2011.

I buy plastic to feel
normal after running my hand

along the Madison grass,
searching for particular grass
no different from the rest
in a 'concerted effort' to break a pattern

all the barking days.

TRUANT

What I loved, seen
through the haze of exhaust:
apartment complexes
at the foot of the valley
where we lived, all of us
walking occasionally
across a hot parking lot
for chicken and cleaning products.
What I feared, knowing
sundown,
100 pages,
every letter of the alphabet
is the universe conspiring with me,
organic machine for my ascension –
I don't give up on it.
I put salad in a jar,
it's my relationship with myself.
We listen a third time.
We hear an augmented fourth.
We see gesture go starward,
sidereal fifth position
over Sundance Plaza, each
future shuttling into another.

GLEAM

I sit in air shaped like a room.

A reflective surface conveys abstract meaning to me.

When we were young we used to live so close to it.

Driving away in an emotional car.

I drink fluoridated tap water.

It doesn't have to be like this.

I can make decisions about the past or throw a party.

It's time to take charge and paint without being judgemental.

My hand out the window of this poem, riding the air.

I won't overemphasize the perfect.

MY BEAUTIFUL HEART COMES AND GOES

I could be blossoming under iron beams
or stuck in traffic with love
in my inbox. I could be
destroying our foundation
with no thoughts or rehearsals
at the hard, sweet centre of life,
treading air-paths for June rain
alone. Weightless. Vertigo
of the imminent future
from this diffuse edge
we ride, one eye slouching
toward betterment, one eye
wrapped in wool and radiant
under the abattoir,
a false star. Some horror leaks in
when we reach the seabed of intimacy,
then it drops again cunningly
into your plastic jewellry.

JARRY PARK

The Academy for Deaf Mutes
suggested I get a haircut.
Then I was at the park, where I got a haircut.

Sparrows nipped a little off the top.
The sharp light reflecting off the pond
shaved the back of my neck.

The sky was experimenting with futurism
in my haircut when I sneezed.
The Park Supervisor thumbed his anti-haircut bylaw.

I wanted the Mount Royal Tennis Club
to observe the progress of my haircut
but the willow tree shielded me from view.

I thought the willow tree could use a haircut.

The pond thought the joggers were a people parade.
I asked the ducks who work in teams what they thought.
Ten ducks counted one haircut then fell asleep.

AUGUST SLOUGH

I did not go with the rest of the class
to see the meteor shower.

It happened anyway.

It's difficult to be at the bar
and to be a lilac bush simultaneously.
I followed a rabbit made of light

along the train tracks.
Don't go there. Say hi

to the image for me. The sun is always
teabagging me. It's art
movie night at Guillaume's.

The after-party attendee thought my books
were a cake? Yes,

I would like a glitter gradient.
My friend Kaity is in a band called Lungbutter.
Do starfish dream of squares?

Do I overshare by holding back?

It's my neighbour's most languorous
Fiat weekend.

If Henrika's ankle were here
I'd suck on it.
We go together like water.

DUMB BODY

I placed my hand against the screen door
to feel the temperature of the air outside.
It was warm.

I left when night felt permanent,
the way a letter gets pulled from an envelope.
The grass was wet

which was significant for vague reasons.
It was everything just to be outside.
Looking up was inspiration

for the stars to do modern dance.
The one where they move
and don't move at the same time.

I was trying to engender gold
in the shape of a time and place.
May something, two thousand something,

when I was moored to distance.
Contact was as thrilling as the fear
that I was having a general experience.

VANISHING FROM YOURSELF

If the end of August knows anything,
it's how to close the door
and sigh. Circumstance rushes
into focus, ceases
swimming in your life-sized aperture.
You've made an arrangement
with existence to be
mostly language, and here
are the results: an impossible
demand for expressivity,
cognitive dissonance. Each word moves
through the liquid universe,
disturbing the calm. At the border,
men with Heckler & Koch
P2000 double action pistols
modified for law enforcement
pressure you into laughing
at a sexist joke in exchange for entry
into the United States. A cone
of burned incense, you collapse
in apartment 3F. Miles of asphalt,
stories of steel. Cars. Exhaust.
History, the dissonance
of the North American continent
swells, the liquid universe roils.
Your Uber arrives in four minutes.
Seven p.m. wraps you in its rosy authority
and likes all your posts. Amy sings,
Love is the hardest art /
You make it in your heart /
Out of nothing. Oil and Coca-Cola linger
on the poisoned lip of the twenty-first century.
The ecstatic prince chews a gold coin.
You dally and ruin, your daily

practice a halo that straddles
two lanes of thought while magnolias
bloom on private property with reality
in the pollen, and red clay
in the pollen, and other magnolias
in the pollen, but you missed the flowers
because you thought about pollen
instead of knowing they are there,
biodegradable like you. The building
you live in is split into rooms for rent,
the body you live in split into skills
for rent. A concentrated pressure
builds at the base of your neck
and you remind yourself to look up,
maybe lie on the floor
and look up at the underside
of the kitchen table, just to not
know for a minute.

CECILIA PAVÓN

I live and breathe
as in a dream
where my roommate moves out,
taking all her parakeets with her.
Of course, she never had any,
but now neither do I.

Oxygen in the blood
of the veins of today, I flow
to and from distinct pulses.
There's a heart in the sky
but all the blinds are drawn:
this is the general set-up.

Discover a symbol
for truth, then obstruct it
with the truth itself.
Ordinary as a flash flood
or clearance sale, and as spectacular,
for a limited time only.

HÔTEL-DIEU

What a great open wound a day can be.

Destiny falters at a moody clip
down St. Dominique

in light's after-party.
No demands for swift

and central momentum,
I only wish I were myself.

For a moment

the gauze is tight, but it isn't
there, around your left hand.

Night drags its feet
outside de Gaspé lofts,

with a mountain in the distance
and a planet in the distance.

TOWN OF MOUNT ROYAL

The laundry machine is on
and it's raining. That's the New Balance
shoe I was talking about.

What separates one building from another
is out of the office until Tuesday.
Can we get some mirrors in here?

Even three differently shaped bowls
on a tray can herald the tinsel train.
Going outside is the only way

to have anything interesting to say
about interior design.
That experience is a sphere

and not a ladder is fundamental.
Hey, c'mon, we've got to finish this pineapple.
Lessons in perspective taught lineation

how to say please and thank you.
The bull of the electric socket.
'The Gardener'

accidentally made a bouquet
of yard clippings.
And But So Yeah!

is my favourite DFW cover band.
I integrated the community spirit
of the commercial into my personality.

You are my ninth-grade boyfriend
sleeping like sunlight in my nail beds.
I can't even.

FLOOD STORY

What I thought were the wracks
of my neighbour's sobs
was just the water main
gushing through concrete.

I think a part of me
was expecting the flood.
A corrupt part of me.
The warning signal was loud enough,
we kept hearing the noise.

Every wave feels like a new wave
rather than a continuation of water.
I'm already sitting here,
a hotel for minerals.

MIRACLES ACKNOWLEDGED ME

Change was from blue to grey,
like a slow-moving traffic signal

on Neptune. The bridge at night
promises promises. To see sound,

draw fireworks with eyes closed.
To feel taste, search for dice

made of blue air behind every sugar bowl
in every renovated kitchen.

The small miracle of mass transit
at night with headphones.

NO WONDER

Between rainy brick buildings,
I take a picture of the roof
of Carnicería Mundial reflected in a puddle

and it simply makes me sad,
even though I've been trying my whole life.
I've gotten it wrong.
My conviction expires.

I'm not sure what I wanted
or even if I wanted it,

but I want to know what I might have wanted,
which is a third order of wanting,
like how a rainbow becomes white light
after it travels through a prism.

Waiting tables at Fresh and Fabulous Pizza
is something that happened
at a point in time.

It's not why –
inclusive of all possible interpretations
from therapists, psychics, and children –

I stand outside the Art Gallery of Ontario

knowing a grey unburst ball of fur will hover,
while a recurring mild insomnia
with no answers
and small questions
reminds me,

day in,
day out,
of the year

I lost before I even possessed it,
the years

that evanesced inside the thrill of arrival,
like a sculpture that cracks
upon being unveiled

or a libidinal desire for destruction
that freezes over the ashes imperceptibly.

The cost of going back is days of rejected influence.

Peopling the sidewalk
after catching up with a dead friend
at a purposefully unfashionable restaurant,
I feel nervous.

She doesn't believe in linear time, she quit acting
because the director of *Dog Sees God*
started to give her confusing instructions, like:

Be yourself.
Act normal.

And in pinioning key life moments,
a sediment settles to the bottom of an underground lake
once and for all.
It cannot be retrieved,

but for the first time
ugly details have kitsch,

and I parade them down peaceful streets
named after violent men.

Before you know it,
you're one more cartoon throwing
Acme Black Holes onto the wall that go nowhere
while birds disappear through them.

THIS PLACE CONTINUES

No matter how
lonely you were

in Peru, this place
continues not to echo
with consequence

or broad pride in a job
well done. Years later,

you buy that yellow
coat. It changes
the way I breathe.

At the end of the year with my bags asking to be let in to the present. Single-family detached homes with comparable square footage curve gradually with the cul-de-sac, as usual. *Did you see the addition to the business park?* Nothing hurts like not being in on the joke. My friends tell me I have a tendency to distance myself from friends, which is troubling. Walking home involved a Walmart, an overpass, a business park, real estate, a Catholic elementary school, and a cosmic sense of purpose determined by faulty or burnt-out street lamps. This is how I remember it: I learned geometry from rooftops. I might carry my laptop onto the back deck in the morning with a cup of coffee and consider how a rainbow's favourite high is gasoline. I might be closer to what I was walking toward and further from where I wanted to be. I'm unsure if the leaves are a part of the plan. Airport security said, *The easiest way out is to look for an entrance.*

UPCYCLE

I.

I remind myself to exist
in the everlasting present

drafting an email
to a potential employer in my head,
subject line:

Every Brand Has a Story –
Here's Mine.

I remind myself instead,

The wind hitting my body cannot be
said to have a beginning or an end,

or, *Guys in bright shoes are playing soccer*
on the astroturf at Alma and St. Zotique,

or, *Choose a job that you love*
and you will never have to work a day in your life,

hopeless though it is,
like an inner tube at a pool party
nostalgic for asphalt.

I'm worried about it now,
the fact that I expect the day to go wrong
so often that when it does
it does not seem wrong at all,

only another variation in the long event
that I react to calmly
and with detached humour

while I search for a more affordable phone service provider,
wasting time being surprised
by the manipulative psychology
of my lemon ginger tea:

Caution! The beverage you are about to enjoy –

It's not enough
to type a destination into Google Maps,

I always end up
with a Street View of Chipotle Mexican Grill
in 3D-rendered Midtown,

but a surge of love
comes while reading a recipe for Dragon Bowls:

> - *Red cabbage*
> - *Daikon*
> - *Sunflower sprouts*
> - *Carrot*
> - *Beets*

gone already
and I sit with the error
that is increasingly hard to recognize,

like a rotating cast of symbols
or affects I can feel the borders of,
pushing against the pelican wall,
chanting,

BE
YOU

BE
YOU

BE
YOU

TIFUL

when I'm drinking alone in Jarry Park
being me,

a philosophy I grasped better as a teenage Taoist
choosing not to smoke pot at lunch
in high school, though I wasn't having 'fun' *per se*,

stumbling heavy with direction and magnitude
into High Def spherical rooms,

like when reading Rilke in translation
and continuing onto the verso
reißt durch beide Bereiche alle Alter –

the palpable spectra without me
on the corner of Alma and St. Zotique.

2.

You have in your head
a few notes of a tune
but you don't know what it is.

If you hum it, it ends
up becoming a different song.

ABSENT REFERENT

Civic arc of overpasses
hurtling toward me –
'Here I am'

using non sequiturs and air quotes.
When I named my sincerity
after a joke it was funny, I guess

you had to be there.
From far away
I saw them and I saw they

were bathed in hindsight,
they were small disturbances
in the surrounding air, I was

bursting with restraint.
My blood and I one
of water's red intervals.

ENTER AND RETURN AS SYNONYMS

I ride my bike on a cold night
five years ago. The future
in which I find myself
instantly is circumspect:
a singing bowl
full of pocket change,
Céline Dion in Mandarin
under the motorized sky,
a microclimate where the sea
is both there and not,
cars like stars, rowing
black air into a disappearing
line that snakes
through five years. I always
ride my bike on a cold night
between rivers who know
there are only two types
of bridge: the bridge we build
to span a distance,
and the bridge we build
to extend one. The present
is not further along a line,
only the sensation
of moving deeper sideways.

LIVE LAUGH LOVE

Rain is frozen in its own shape.

Heart on the trees.

Nevada is Spanish

for snowfall.

Whatever I see is.

I wear my pills.

Some light patterning.

Sophistry of the elite.

Are you always

envisioning a path?

Do ancient representations

of grain stir you?

One that is somehow not.

Generous meteor

can I kiss the distant artificial light

can't you come come

can't you be here

pressing hard on sunbeams.

Cutting up the no.

Restrictions apply.

Lesser stars.

Progress the accidental

success of greed.

Sensation of

Crystal Palace.

Visualization of thought

before motion pictures.

What one does is not

what two do.

Head a delicate

helmeted heart.

Bubble of tasty static.

Black horse going aquatic.

Up quark.

Charm quark.

Advanced Pottery.

Touch tone.

HOLIDAY

Under the football stadium,
far away from myself. The demolition team
arrived before I was awake.

They demolished my sleep. Some giants
took a pair of scissors to the clouds,
turning every threshold into a snowport.

There were auguries of a new living arrangement
between the italics on the drive-thru sign.
Canned peaches in light

syrup on a sheet-metal shelf at the gas station
waited patiently for acceptance.
I wept

taciturnly, meaning I was cruel
in the interest of protection
on a bus named after a famously grey dog.

Tonight you are fuming at me
while reading the biography of Zora Neale Hurston
and outside the snow
removal trucks carve diesel
paths through the streets
while I circle condensed nothing.
It's February.
My mind is cloven.
Above the engines and nothing
I can hear, as if from the end
of a long, underground tunnel,
the familiar chords of a hymn,
but the hymn is not
being sung in English
or in French, it is not
in a language I understand,
and the piano – the chords
are being played on a piano –
is out of tune
and in listening I am no longer
'reading next to you in bed,'
not taken out of context
like a quotation and inserted
into a narrative I do not recognize –
I am not that, I am
only what can be articulated
in negatives, a lost item
that is definitely not there,
its location possessed wholly
by its self, a symbol
for what is unknown
rather than not knowing –
the source text
coming to life in real time.

The difference between
a normal person
and an exceptional person
is the willingness to be seen
as abnormal, you say. The piano
player's foot on the soft pedal.
Hurston refused to attend graduate
classes at Columbia
and lost half her Guggenheim
grant as a result, then travelled
to Haiti and wrote
Their Eyes Were Watching God
in fifty-six days, in a single draft.
I try to look impressed, but
it comes off stoic and sarcastic.
Smoking weed together in the bath
forty minutes ago, you
carved out my cruelty
and held it in the palm of your eye:
one minute I'm concussed
with affection, the next
I make a stoic and sarcastic
facial expression, then glance
to the side after you speak.
Lacking specificity for my regret,
I read aloud a sentence
from *Giovanni's Room*:
With this fleeting thought
there came another, equally fleeting:
a new sense of Giovanni,
his private life and pain,
and all that moved
like a flood in him
when we lay together at night.

The symbol mutates again,
into an absurd state
made inevitable by the shadow
of its predecessor.
In my hurry to be forgiven
I omitted what fires his empathy,
Giovanni's *Oui, monsieur*,
and I think of you saying
Oui, monsieur, at the bookstore,
my heart's sudden heaviness,
how it's hidden from you.
I wonder if David allows himself to be
concussed with affection
because his love will remain
forever incorporeal,
his sincerity only made possible
by the impossibility
of proving it to Giovanni.
All night I've been circling
condensed nothing in this way,
trying to narrow the distance
between an image of the world
and my experience of it:
the events that inform a book,
its contents, your interpretation,
mine, the piano player's
foot on the sustain pedal.
Our movable present
is an axis and so appears
to be still as we turn deeper
into February,
tone layering upon tone
like the falling snow.

ACTION WITHOUT ACTION

Kelvin the dog did not understand,
he just chased his tail
and whined.
I printed my poem out
on a rectangular piece of paper
using the family printer
but that felt disrespectful,
to have something as definite
as a rectangle.
Later Kelvin died
of old age like a pro. Snow

undulates across the wide surface of the on-ramp,
the SUV spins out.
Some voices on the radio have opinions
on the war in Afghanistan.
Expecting laws
written for Prisoners of War
from World War II
to protect detainees today
is like putting a basketball court
on the moon and expecting
the same number of dunks.

My father drove,
I used magical thinking
to keep an accident away
on the wide surface of the on-ramp.

CHEER UP, JAY RITCHIE

Weeks go by and then
morning is a song

by the Cocteau Twins,
full of incomprehensible psalms.
The army trailer arrives,

young urban creatives laugh,
there is concern
regarding loss of grey matter –

from the plane of the Ubisoft aprons
the twenty-first century exhales.

Leafless tree, I'm hallucinating.

The army trailer departs,
the coffee is bitter,

November was a painting
I looked at but didn't
share any thoughts on
after we rendezvoused.

Beauty is proportional to distance.
Walk away to get close.

And I will think about inevitability,
how it's beautiful anyway,
that such a structure can exist at all,
that we go along with it,
that we're the ones who shape it,
that seasons come and go no matter what,
that it's under new management,

that yesterday is over,
that nothing, not even death, is certain,
that heaven came down and kissed me,
and it's funny how it's funny,

how time moves fast then stops,
how the long way can be the short way,
how giving is easy,
how gratitude is free,
how I believe in everything,
how there are omens if I want them,
how fragile and heavy the hum.

NO SPRINGS HONEST WEIGHT

Distant hum of a generator
         rising between windrows.

High on exercise, I walk
         between the left and right eye

of the beast whose face is so wide
         you can't see it all at once.

Winter is a homeward corridor.

HORROR MOVIE IN WHICH THE AIR IS THE MONSTER

I.

You never knew an emergency
could move so slowly. All day the pines
stood indolent, repeating their mantra
go go go and so you – go, past the Centre
of Hope where Emily won a prize
for volunteer initiatives, past cartoon cities
made of crystals in the frost on a sideview mirror,
past breaking down.

Vishal is making calls, administering the flow
of night into bodies. Limpidity exists between
where you said you were going to be
and where you are.

2.

     When I wake up,
the sounds are
     covered in snow.
On the floor
     with paintings

     from the thrift store.
I navigate between
     sleeping bodies like a fish
around a wreck.
     Joy hides a black circle

     under my tongue.
The river chases itself
     in circles, the riverbed
reads the collected works
     of clouds.

THE WAY THE WATER IS VS. THE WAY THE WATER WAS

I am going to a funeral.
There are no other
options. Pomegranates
are on sale. I saw
them when I left

The Bottle Depot, seven dollars
forty-five cents
in my pocket.
They made me
hungry. I have never

been to this part of town
before. It is said
that the spirit
fights hard for many
years using its Arsenal.

Oh wow, a bonsai tree.
But ultimately the Arsenal
is taken from the spirit
and balance
is restored. Even water

gets existential
when it snows. When
I woke up I turned
on my iPod. The straight-edge
kids were eating glass.

Only four people
can fit in the car
and go to Taco Time.
I want a Mexi-Fries
Deluxe Combo,

those are good.
It is further said that
the Arsenal is then
dismantled and scattered
in the physical realm.

CELEBRATION OF LIFE

Every mourner was given
a blue, yellow,
or green helium-filled balloon
and was pushed out
into the snow-covered field.
Releasing the balloon
into the troposphere
was a symbolic gesture
for the final stage
in the grieving process:
acceptance, or 'letting go.'
How many leatherback
turtles are going to die

from this mass act of littering?
I had done a project on
leatherbacks in Grade 7.
It was the fourth consecutive day
of putting my suit on, and the fourth
consecutive day of putting
ice cream in my coffee.
Three people had died
in one day, and for three days
there was one funeral per day –
except today is different, today
is a celebration of life.
I unparked the suv

from the half-frozen mud.
What is going to happen
to everyone's nice shoes?
The nonsmokers look so natural
holding their cigarettes.
I wanted to clarify some negative

comments I had made, but I did not
expect to encounter absence,
which is no encounter at all,
just a persistent humming
at the highest audible register
and its root note at the lowest,
making a chord

with idling city maintenance
vehicles. The possibility
that photographs would be
insufficient occurred to everyone
at once, it was unanimously decided
someone would make a DVD.
The Rocky Mountains
had a better understanding
of us, they had seen
the oil barons as heroes
and were less anxious, they said,
Squint, you can see tomorrow
through tiny pinholes in the air.

CLICKABLE INTERIOR

I put on my noise-cancelling headphones.
Silence makes my bedroom bigger:

A planet where I am the core.
The city is a distant star.

I remember a word I do not know.
I look it up in my e-dictionary:

A literal quasar is my figurative lodestar.

The city is an asterisk (star, 2nd def.).
Funny that I can minimize a window.

The title 'In Watermelon Sugar' is borrowed from the novel of the same name by Richard Brautigan. The image of 'remaining trout' in the poem is borrowed from 'Short Talk on Trout' by Anne Carson.

'Multi-Level Marketing' borrows a phrase from a piece of public art by Caroline Caldwell, the title of a mixed-media artwork by Mark Bradford, and a phrase from a Lululemon bag.

'Gleam' borrows a lyric from the song 'REALiTi' by Grimes.

The italicized lines in 'Vanishing from Yourself' were sung by Amy McDaniel during a reading at Mammal Gallery in Atlanta, August 2016.

'Flood Story' contains an excerpt from the Akkadian epic *Atrahasis* (translated by S. Dalley).

'No Wonder' borrows the image of 'a grey ball of fur' from *Sula* by Toni Morrison.

Part one of 'Upcycle' contains an excerpt from *Duino Elegies* by Rainer Maria Rilke, a phrase attributed to Confucius, and the warning printed on Starbucks cups.

Part two of 'Upcycle' is an excerpt from an interview with Elena Ferrante conducted by *The Paris Review* (The Art of Fiction No. 228).

'Softcover' contains an excerpt from *Giovanni's Room* by James Baldwin.

'No Springs, Honest Weight' was the official slogan of the Toledo Scale Company.

ACKNOWLEDGMENTS

Heartfelt thanks to the editors of the following journals, where versions of some of these poems first appeared: *glitterMOB*, *Spork*, *The Puritan*, *Vallum*, *carte blanche*, *Powder Keg*, and *Bad Nudes*.

I want to thank everyone at Coach House, especially my editor Jeramy Dodds, for his encouragement and attentiveness; the extended Metatron family; Drawn & Quarterly publishers and bookstore staff, for their relentless support; my patient and multi-talented friend Marcela Huerta, for creating the cover; my parents.

For your conversation and brilliance, thank you: Ashley Opheim, Guillaume Morissette, David Walker, Monica Mc-Clure, Zoe Sharpe, A. Zachary.

The book is dedicated to Henrika Larochelle, for her honesty, support, and insight.

Typeset in Brandon Grotesque and Aragon.

Printed at Coach House on bpNichol Lane in Toronto, Ontario, on Zephyr Antique Laid paper, which was manufactured, acid-free, in Saint-Jérôme, Quebec, from second-growth forests. This book was printed with vegetable-based ink on a 1973 Heidelberg KORD offset litho press. Its pages were folded on a Baumfolder, gathered by hand, bound on a Sulby Auto-Minabinda and trimmed on a Polar single-knife cutter.

Edited by Jeramy Dodds
Designed by Norman Nehmetallah
Cover design by Marcela Huerta
Author photo by Stacy Lee

Coach House Books
80 bpNichol Lane
Toronto ON M5S 3J4
Canada

416 979 2217
800 367 6360

mail@chbooks.com
www.chbooks.com